Contemplating Sophia
Pursuing Wisdom

Rev Colleen Kite

for

Andrew, Sarah,

&

Matthew

Contents

The Biblical and other quotations in the text are in this font. The references are in the Notes. The Reader can probably apply them appropriately but, if not, it is not disadvantageous. They are here to achieve academic rigour in an unacademic way.

My thoughts are in this font.

The Lady's Prayer

Holy Sophia,
Who comes from God, who gives birth to God,
Who is God,
Who is ever present and all knowing,
we thank you for Your all-encompassing presence.
We recognise those times when we received Your comfort and support.
We thank you that You gave us assistance during our difficulties
that were created either by others or by ourselves.

Holy Sophia,
we also remember those times when we felt Your absence;
when we were in need of protection or comfort
and we saw no care or support.
Help us to understand, and to forgive those who offended against us.
And, if this feels to be beyond us at this time,
help us to accept and find accommodation within our difficulties and to lay no blame on either Your Self or on our selves.

Holy Sophia,
aid us, we ask, on our journey through life.
Help us to find a knowledge and awareness of you
in both your gentle and forceful aspects.
May we journey together for yours is the way, the truth and the life.
Amen

A Prayer of Dedication

Holy Sophia, divine Mashiakh,
accept our prayers, we ask,
as we place ourselves before You.

Life has many twists and turns but it always returns
to You.
May we benefit from the good choices we make;
may we learn from our mistakes.
You send us love to support us, teachers to lead us.
You allow us challenges to strengthen us.
For this, we thank You.

Our time here on Earth is for becoming closer to You.
It is now time to look toward You
by looking away from You
and seeing You in the world around us.
As above so below.

As we look around us, we see suffering, hunger,
ignorance... We also see fruitfulness, kindness,
compassion...
Help us to understand that we cannot contain the
sorrow, relinquish the pain, alleviate the suffering.

We see You – in the goodness and in the bad, in the
fullness and in the lack.
May we be grateful throughout the best and the worst
of times.
We can serve, not only in material ways, but also by
acknowledging Your presence, by asking for Your help,
support and guidance.

May we confirm our desire to serve You and find our true purpose in this life.

May we each echo the words of Miriam Hannah,

'Behold, the servant of the Lord; be it unto me according to thy word.'

> hey eney am'tah d'metia
> neheya lay ayach meletach

ܡܐ ܐܢܐ ܐܡܬܐ ܐܢܐ ܗܐ ܕܡܬܐ

d'metia am'tah eney hey

ܢܗܐ ܠܝ ܐܝܟ ܡܠܬܟ,

meletach ayach lay neheya

הא אנא אמתה דמתיא
d'metia am'tah eney hey

נהוא לי איך מלתך
meletach ayach lay neheya

A Story of Noah that wasn't included in the Bible

4000 BCE

Genesis 6

Noah was a good man; he loved his wife with whom he had three sons: Shem, Ham and Japheth. He worked hard tilling the ground and raising animals.

However, most of his countrymen were not so good. They were lazy and didn't repair the drainage channels for the crops. They spent their time with other men's wives and daughters and were belligerent when asked to work. Their parties were out of this world.

Consequently, Noah's land was suffering from extreme drought. The crops began to fail and no-one would help Noah to work in the fields.
So, Noah said to God, 'Please, God, send me rain. The crops have failed again and we are starving. My family will die if we don't get rain. Please, please, please send me rain.'
God replied, 'You are a good man, Noah, but your countrymen have been lazy, wicked and uncaring. But I hear your pleas - I will send you rain.'

The rest is history: it rained; Noah sheltered in the ark; he sent out a raven to test the waters; he then sent out doves, the symbol of compassion. And Noah survived and turned to God to thank him whereupon God promised never to send such rain again. We have the rainbow to this day to remind us of the commitment between Noah and God.

And God said, 'Replenish the Earth and, next time, it will be better for you to sort out your own problems first.'

March 2020 CE

Apocalypse 1

Noah is a good man; he and his wife work hard and are bringing up their children to be good people. They work hard, support Friends of the Earth, recycle properly and grow their own vegetables.

However, most of his countrymen are not so good. They are lazy and rely on the dole when work is short. When employed, they get what else they can by photocopying personal work in the office or by claiming extra mileage allowance. They enjoy other people's company, men or women - life is more advanced now, anything goes. Their parties are out of this world - alcohol is cheap and other drugs are readily available. They are multiplying and replenishing the earth - with humans; and depleting the earth of resources.

The animals and plants are suffering at our hands, and we are eating anything and everything to the point of extinction.

Replenish the earth? We are denuding it.

And Noah says, 'Please, God, heal the earth. We are suffocating from bad air and our resources are short. Please, please, please, heal our earth.'
The environmentalists say, 'Please, heal the earth. Stop making plastics, stop filling landfill sites, stop

exterminating animals. Please, please, please, heal our earth.'

God replied, 'You are a good man Noah but your countrymen have been lazy, wicked and uncaring. But I hear your pleas - I will heal your earth.'

The rest will soon be history: poverty, Covid, disease, suffering ...

Noah will shelter in his ark of isolation and on-line shopping.
When he releases his doves of compassion, he will see that the earth is healing. The landfills will reduce with lower consumption; dolphins will swim in the Venice lagoon, the San Francisco fog will clear, nitrogen dioxide levels will decrease in cities.

Noah will survive; the environmentalists will survive.

Will anyone thank God? Will anyone be grateful that our earth has healed through human beings being made to act responsibly?
What will our rainbow be like?
And God and the environmentalists will say,
'Next time, sort out your own problems yourselves first.'

August 2020

Apocalypse continues

Noah Junior to his father: Dad, can I go out to play football?
Noah: Yes son, but don't forget social distancing. Stay away from the other players.
Noah Junior: What! No tackling then?
Noah: No, it's best not to tackle. And don't forget to wear a mask.
Noah Junior: What! I can't shout at them then?
Noah: No. No tackling and no shouting at them.
Noah Junior: Alright. I'll just get my football...
Noah: Don't forget your hand gel. If anyone touches the ball you should use your hand cleanser.
Noah Junior: Right. No tackling; no shouting, no touching the ball. Dad, can I play on your games box instead?

Spring 2021

Spring: the trees are greening, the flowers are flowering, and the people are emerging from isolation.

We have the vaccine to protect us. Our health care workers have looked after us; our scientists have created our vaccines; the essential services have continued despite their many challenges.

We are emerging from solitude, desolation, from whatever our personal experience was during this time. And now we must connect with our fellow human beings: safely and sensitively.

We must listen to our Earth, to our God by whatever name he is known, to the environmentalists.

Can we stop this from ever happening again?

Will there be another Apocalypse?
When will it be: next year? in ten years?
What will we do about it?

~~The Creed~~ My Creed

A dog is for life not just Christmas
However
A creed is for now, neither just for Christmas nor for life

Being a Christian usually involves belonging to or joining a church; each church has its own set of beliefs whether it's called a creed or not. And then the organization becomes petrified, having a rock-solid set of statements which cannot be changed or developed without much discussion and agreement amongst the governing body. The Ten Commandments inscribed on stone and the Smaragdine Tablet etched onto an emerald are good examples of such statements.

It seems to me that a creed should be a living, evolving set of ideas which develops as understanding grows. No two members of a community are likely to be at the same stage of the journey through life, so it is a worthwhile practice to create one's own creed to which one can relate with complete agreement both intellectually and emotionally.

Here's my creed for today. It is not what I would have written ten years ago nor will write in the future. Yours will be different...

My Creed

I acknowledge:
There is a Universal Energy which continually creates our universe: an Energy which constructs, sustains and destructs as appropriate.

Life is a progression towards an understanding of and becoming united with this Energy; many are those who have achieved this understanding: Yeshua, the Buddha, Guru Nanak, Mohammed ... they are enlightened, awake, saints in this world.

There are many aspects to this Energy: the divine feminine as Sophia (in her many guises as Mary the Magdalene, the Theotokos...); the divine masculine as the Father, the Son; the Holy Spirit; love, compassion, strength...

Every human being is a Son or Daughter of this Energy and each one has the potential to experience oneness with It.

I accept the two Testaments as spiritual writing to be understood spiritually; I also accept the value of non-canonical texts.

Life on Earth is dualistic and both aspects need to be addressed: its materialistic and spiritual aspects; the active and the passive; service and contemplation;, apophatic and cataphatic practice.

Eventually the two practices become as one, a unified life in Divine Energy.

The Sacraments of Holy Qurbana, Baptism, Confirmation, Chrismation, Redemption, Matrimony and Ordination exist for our support and comfort and are voluntary practices. However, it is of benefit to us to partake regularly of the Holy Qurbana to reaffirm our alignment with the divine and our willingness to serve the Holy Energy.

The spirituality of Yeshua / Jesus was one of blessing. We are all blessed ...

Your Creed

The Lord's Prayer

Our Father
Who art in Heaven
hallowed be Thy name.
Thy kingdom come,
Thy will be done
on Earth as it is in Heaven.
Give us this day our daily bread
and forgive us our trespasses as we forgive those who
trespass against us.
Lead us not into temptation,
but deliver us from evil.
for Thine is the kingdom, the power and the glory,
For ever and ever, Amen.

The Lord's Prayer

Abba - divine Father, divine Mother, O Thou
who lives in Heaven, in that place within us all if only
we listen, accept and have faith
Abba Abboun - our divine One, not mine but ours. We
pray for and on behalf of all your people.
May Your name be set apart, revered, sanctified, as
Your name is held by You alone. Let it not be mis-used
in meaningless chatter.
May Your sovereignty, Your care and Your overarching
vision, be accepted throughout the Earth, within the
hearts and minds of all peoples, within that Heaven
which is within us all.
Allow us nourishment both materially and spiritually
so that each day we become more like You and channel
Your love more freely.
Forgive us when we do wrong in thought or action,
when we fall short through our own personal error.
Forgive us when we do nothing when there was
something we should or could have done.
Sometimes we fall short; help us to recognise that
others do too and to not hold resentment when we feel
aggrieved at the actions or words of others.
Help us all to do and think rightly; help us to not do
or think what we know to be wrong.
Protect us on our journey through life so that we may
become one with You in Your sovereignty, Your
strength and Your majestic beauty.
May You live with and within us all for timeless
eternity. So be it.
Amen.

The Healing Prayer

Holy Sophia
we thank You for Your presence and support in times past.
Be with us now, we ask, in this time of need.
We ask for Your help and that of Archangel Raphael.
May Your healing energies flow throughout the earth plane
to all those who have asked for Your help.
Remember all those whose names are written in the healing books
Of us, Your followers.
We ask for support and healing especially for ...

Holy Sophia
remember also those who are not known to us
but who are in need of help or support;
those who, perhaps, do not understand
that Your help is ready for those who ask.

And if our path requires us to live the challenges that face us,
help us,
Holy Sophia, to bear the troubles with patience and understanding.
May we grow in health and strength
in the knowledge of the High Father, the Divine Mother and the Everlasting Son.
Amen

Creation 1

In the beginning God created (ברא bârâ') the heavens
and the earth.

*Emanation. The continual outpouring of energy in
the continuing now.*
*There is no beginning. Time doesn't exist. It is a
chimera, a fantasy, a dream. We exist now; we
existed in the past; we will exist in the future. Now
always exists.*
*Change happens. Creation involves change from one
state to another.*
*Change happens. The heavens come and go and come
again.*

And the earth was without form and empty. And
darkness was on the face of the deep. And the Spirit of
God moved upon the face of the waters.

Emptiness. Vacuité. Śūnyatā.
Not desolation, but an Emptiness full of potential.
*Emptiness awaiting the spark of ignition. Emptiness
awaiting Life. Atzilut.*
Darkness; the absence of light; absence of the Light.
*Sophia of the ělôhîym, conceives of existence and
nurtures it, releasing it from the womb of deep
waters.*

And God said, 'Let there be light.' And there was light.
And God saw that the light was good. And God divided
the light from the darkness. And God called the light,
Day. And He called the darkness, Night. And the
evening and the morning were the first day.

The divine energy moved as sound, creating light, a higher vibration. Light is good. With light comes knowledge, wisdom and understanding: Da'at, Chokmâh, and Binah.

Darkness is not bad. It allows for rest in the divine. Consolidation.

Day and night; the ceaseless round of created time allowing the opportunity to both shine and rest. Evening comes first, then Day. We rest in spirit first, then we shine. Time is born - a convention that helps us to notice change. If we exist within time, we postulate, we have a reality, a permanence. And we will have an end. Day 1

And God said, 'Let there be a firmament in the middle of the waters, and let it divide the waters from the waters.' And God made the firmament ... and called the firmament, Heaven. And the evening and the morning were the second day.

Divine energy moved again creating the firmament above, a great arch of heavens, in which future mankind could envisage the home of the elôhîym. We need something to look up to, to respect, to aspire to. At first, the elôhîym are above us. As we evolve and learn, we realize the elôhîym are all around and within us. Day 2

And God said, 'Let the waters under the heaven be gathered together to one place and be called seas; and let the dry land appear; and be called Earth. Let the earth bring forth tender sprouts upon the earth, the herb seeding seed, the fruit tree producing fruit after its kind, whose seed is in itself;' and it was so. And God saw that it was good. And the evening and the morning were the third day.

Divine energy set the land apart from the waters naming them earth and seas. Naming is an important action; it assigns ownership, indicates control but also implies protection and support, a responsibility to care. It was good. Everything the elôhíym does is good. Day 3

And God said, 'Let there be lights in the heavens to divide the day from the night. And let them be for signs, and for seasons, and for days and years.' ... And it was so. And God made two great lights: the greater light to rule the day and the smaller light to rule the night, and the stars also ... And God saw that it was good. And the evening and the morning were the fourth day.

Divine energy placed the stars in the night sky for light in the darkness but also to mark the seasons and years, a necessary facet of an agricultural society. Not only can we notice, record and predict time's movement, but we can use that knowledge for our benefit. Also, the sun and moon were placed to rule over day and night. The sun with its strong, masculine nature and the moon with a much more feminine character. She runs her own course in her own way, and in her own time. While she rules the night, she also appears on occasion during the day. Her influence is subtle, strong; it has her own special regularity as seen in the tides. It was good - of course. Everything the elôhíym does is good. Day 4

And God said, 'Let the waters swarm with creatures having a living soul; and let birds fly over the earth on the face of the heavens.' And God created great sea-animals, and every living soul that creeps with which the waters swarmed after their kind; and every winged fowl after its kind. And God saw that it was good.

And God blessed them, saying, 'Be fruitful and multiply, and fill the waters of the seas and let the fowl multiply in the earth.' And the evening and the morning were the fifth day.

The elôhîym now instructed and enabled the populating of both land and sea with creatures having soul, נֶפֶשׁ, nephesh. Sea life great and small, land creatures and birds have nephesh. We should remember this; animals have souls too. Each creature has its sphere in which it should stay - the sea animals in the sea, the fowl in the air. It was good ... Day 5

God said, 'Let the earth bring forth the living creature, the creeping things, and the beasts of the earth after their kind.' And it was so. God saw that it was good.

And God said, 'Let Us make man in Our image, after Our likeness. And let them have dominion over the fish of the sea, the fowl of the heavens, the cattle and over all the creepers creeping on the earth.' And God created man in His image; in the image of God He created him. He created them male and female. And God blessed them. And God said to them, 'Be fruitful, and multiply and fill the earth, and subdue it. And have dominion over the fish of the sea and over the fowl of the heavens, and all animals that move upon the earth.'

And God saw everything that He had made, and behold, it was very good. And the evening and the morning were the sixth day.

The ełôhĭym now encouraged the earth to 'bring forth' mammals; to let them evolve in their own ways.

The scribe seems to have become confused; is God one or many? Our or His? Paradoxes happen.

The ełôhĭym is a paradox, coming from ełôahh אֱלֹהַּ, grammatically feminine, with ĭym masculine plural. A feminine aspect within the deity allowing it a plurality of masculine and feminine? Or is it that our God is greater than a normal singular entity? Paradoxes resolve.

We are to subdue כָּבַשׁ kâbash and have dominion רדה râdâh over nature. We are to subjugate our fellow creatures. Need we do this so completely, so unkindly? When did we forget responsibility or have we not yet acquired it?

It was very good ... Day 6

And on the seventh day God ended His work which He
had made. And He rested on the seventh day from all
His work which He had made. And God blessed the
seventh day and sanctified it, because in it He had
rested from all His work which God created to make.

The ełôhĭym stopped working as the intended creation was complete.
The ełôhĭym 'rested' ...? The heart still beats, the lifeblood still flows. Creation continues in a ceaseless expansion of spirit consciousness.
All potentiality is now created - ברא bârâ'. The ełôhĭym rests within the new creation, the immaterial world, Beriah. It is this world that is very good, Beriah. Day 7

Creation of the immaterial world is complete –
Atzilut and Beriah.

Creation 2

There was not a man to till the ground (ǎdâmâh) but there
went up a mist from the earth (ארץ), and watered the
whole face of the ground (ǎdâmâh). And the LORD God
(יהוה אלהים yehôvâh elôhîym) formed (יצר yâtsar) man
(אדם 'âdâm) of the dust of the ground (ǎdâmâh) and
breathed (נפח nâphach) into his nostrils the breath (נשמה
neshâmâh) of life; and man became a living soul (נפש
nephesh).

*Rain fell and seeded the ground. It also provided the
substance for the creation of mankind; âdâm derived
from ǎdâmâh. At this point man - or better, mankind
- is neither male nor female. Or it is both male and
female. Man - אדם 'âdâm - is a living soul, a nephesh.
It is not yet a physical being but a potential human.
This is the world of Formation, Yetzirah.*

And the Lord God planted a garden in Eden and put
mankind (אדם 'âdâm) that he had formed (יצר yâtsar)
therein. He planted all kinds of trees including the Tree of
Life and the Tree of the Knowledge of Good and Evil.
And the Lord God commanded that mankind dress (עבד
'âbad) it and keep (שמר shâmar) it.

*This is a Yetziratic garden, a spiritual Eden; a paradise
to be cared for and protected.
Mankind was to work the garden and protect it. We
have done the former but the latter? It seems that the
more advanced we become the less we keep the land
in its full meaning. It is ours to guard and protect -
perhaps we are finally beginning to understand this.*

'Of every tree of the garden you may freely eat but of the
Tree of Knowledge of Good and Evil, you shall not eat
because, on that day you shall surely die.'

Adam is alone here; the commandment was given to him/her alone.

The garden was filled with birds and animals but, despite Adam naming them all, not one was suitable as a companion. The Lord God determined to make (âśâh) one.

> And the LORD God caused a deep sleep to fall upon Adam and He took one of his ribs, and made it into a woman. And Adam said, … 'she shall be called Woman (אשה 'ishshâh) because she was taken out of Man (איש 'îysh)'.

Woman was made or built (הנב banah) and they receive new names to replace Adam. Their essence is now different. Now Adam must work with, co-operate with, live with another. This brings both companionship and responsibility.

> The serpent was the most crafty animal that the Lord God had made (עשה 'âśâh). Woman knew she must not eat of the Tree of Knowledge of Good and Evil but the serpent told her, 'You shall surely not die but God knows, that the day you eat thereof, then your eyes shall be opened, and you shall be like gods, knowing good and evil.' And when the woman saw that the tree was … to be desired to make one wise, she took its fruit and did eat, and gave also to her husband who was with her; and he did eat. And the eyes of them both were opened, and they knew that they were naked; and they sewed fig leaves together, and made themselves aprons.

God has made mankind and sent the whisper or hiss (the literal translation of nachash, serpent) knowing that mankind will desire the knowledge available to gods. Woman heard the whisper, listened and desired *the understanding of good and evil. Man followed her without question or challenge, it seems.*

When the Lord God asked why they had disobeyed Him, man blamed woman and woman blamed the serpent. Punishment ensued ... The LORD God made (עשׂה 'âśâh) coats of skin and clothed them. He said, 'Mankind is become like one of us knowing good and evil; and now, in case he also takes from the Tree of Life, and eats, and lives for ever, he must leave Eden'. Adam named woman Eve (חוה chavvâh), life-giver, the mother of all.

They are now man and woman, fysh and ishshâh. They have clothes of skin but realise their nakedness or state of unknowing. They know now that they lack wisdom, they are ignorant in the literal not the pejorative sense. Man was beside Woman at this time. Did he resist or refuse the fruit? It seems not. He happily accepted it. This looks bad but now they have the opportunity to learn wisdom and to voluntarily find their way back to a relationship with the divine.
Was this perhaps the plan all along? To make a creation that voluntarily looked to and reflected the divine? Was the 'serpent' really serving this plan? Can we see the work of Sophia within the serpent? - the final creative act, a being capable of developing a real relationship with the divine?

Sophia creates from beginning to end, Atzilut to Assiyah.

Sophia of the elôhîym, conceives of existence and nurtures it, releasing it from the womb of deep waters. Sophia as 'serpent' enables beings whose eyes are opened, who are able to be like gods, knowing good and evil.

Our skins are made (עָשָׂה 'âśâh). We are now in Assiyah, the world of matter.

Creation of the universe is complete - Atzilut, Beriah, Yetzirah and Assiyah.

The Four Holy Truths of Job

Life is unsatisfactory and consists of much suffering.

Job was a perfect and upright man. He was doing well.
He had seven sons, three daughters, seven thousand
sheep, three thousand camels, five hundred of both
oxen and she asses. What more could he want?
Job worried that his sons did not love and respect God
as he did. So Job prayed that they be sanctified; and
he made sacrifices for them.
And, in time, everything he owned left him through
war, pillage, environmental disaster. But Job was
perfect; he neither blamed God nor himself but
remained at peace and accepting. He still had his
health.
But suffering comes to all, even Job, and he developed
sores from the top of his head to the soles of his feet.
This also he accepted without complaint or desire for
their end.
Job commented, 'Oh, the suffering, from being born,
from growing old, from becoming ill and, in the end,
from dying.'

Job had three friends: Eliphaz, Bildad, and Zophar.
They saw his grief and comforted him.
Eliphaz suggested that for Job to suffer thus he must
have committed some great error. If only Job would
confess to God he would be delivered from his troubles.
But Job still had strength and wisdom and resisted
Eliphaz' accusations of blame and guilt.
Bildad was even less comfort; if Job's children had
sinned and he asked for forgiveness, then surely a just
and worthy God would heal Job who is pure and
upright? But who was Job to challenge God? And why

should God not mete out good and bad to everyone, God fearing or otherwise, in equal measure?

Job's soul was weary of life, its good and its bad. He realised that suffering is integral to the human situation.

Zophar added his support to that of his friends. "Job, you say your doctrine is pure but can you really find out God by searching? There is a way: prepare your heart, put wickedness away and then you will forget your misery." In other words, "Job, it's through your own fault! It's up to you to find your way."

Bildad confirms, "How can a man be right with God? Even the stars are not pure; how much less is mankind who is like a worm."

Job confirmed his intention to follow his path; he would walk in truth and moral integrity. Where can one find wisdom and understanding? By revering God and departing from doing wrong. Despite his old age, ill health and impending death, Job continued in acceptance and non-attachment to both his past wealth and present suffering.

Job prayed for his adversarial friends and received twice his previous wealth in return: fourteen thousand sheep, six thousand camels, and a thousand of both oxen and she asses.

The Four Holy Truths according to Job:
1. Life is suffering and attachment to both the good in life and the bad.
2. Suffering is caused by desire, craving for more of the good and less of the bad.
3. There is a solution to the unsatisfactoriness of life; we do not have to continuously suffer during the vicissitudes of life.

4. The solution is to follow the path which is:
   a. for Job, to revere God and depart from doing wrong;
   b. for the Jew, it is to learn the Torah and follow the Ten Commandments;
   c. for the Christian, it is to pursue 'the way, the truth and the life' of Jesus / Yeshua; and
   d. for the Buddhist, it is to practise the Noble Eightfold Path.

Sophia's Noble Eightfold Path

Blessed is the one who finds Sophia - wisdom, and the
one who gets understanding ... She is more precious than
rubies ... Her ways are ways of pleasantness, and all her
paths are peace.

To the Buddha, wisdom and compassion are necessary
attributes on the path to enlightenment. His eight
paths, which are to be followed simultaneously, aim to
achieve both.

Eight paths:
1. right speech
2. right action
3. right livelihood
4. right effort
5. right mindfulness
6. right concentration
7. right view
8. right resolve

Take each, one at a time, like a cobble and build it into
a pathway; each one is a vital step for the journey.
When all are together, the journey, like a pilgrimage,
has a purpose and a destination.

The eight paths are contained in three highways: those
of ethics, meditation and wisdom. Allow each and all
to permeate your being. The grace of God is given freely
but we need to take steps to receive it and it is
travelling along this eightfold path that facilitates the
taking root of wisdom and compassion in our hearts
and the flourishing of grace.

Ethics

Whatever you would like people to do to you, do so to them.

We are all children of the divine. We all have the spark of divinity within us. So treat the sparks of divinity in others as we would have ours treated.
Sometimes these sparks lie deep beneath the surface; sometimes we have to polish them a little to let them show and our inner divinity will begin to sparkle.

1.   Right speech:

Do not bear false witness against your neighbour, friend or loved one.

Other people have the seed of divinity within them; they are precious to Sophia. They deserve our respect and love. To slander or offend them is to slander or offend Sophia.

You shall not take the name of Jehovah your God in vain.

His name is sacred; as the Jew will not pronounce יהוה or yehôvâh out of respect but use Adonai when reading from the scriptures, so should we consider our use of language in times of stress or frustration.

Blessed are the peacemakers; they shall be called the children of God.

We need peace to thrive and learn, to have time and space to be reverential in whatever way we choose. Peace within ourselves and amongst ourselves.

The sage says little - it is a natural thing to talk sparingly - because even a great wind and lashing rain do not go on for ever.

The less said the better. This is an age of communication, frequently without forethought or consideration of the possible outcomes of idle chatter. Lady Wisdom and the Taoist sage say little.

2. Right action:

You shall not ...

There are so many examples of 'you shall not': kill, commit adultery, steal. They all impact the wellbeing of others and also ourselves. To kill leaves blood on our hands; to be unfaithful denies our integrity; to steal bloats us with the energies of others and tarnishes our purity.

You shall not make a graven image ... You shall not bow yourself down to them, nor serve them ...

Nothing can take the place of the divine - not learning, ritual, television.

But I say to you who hear, 'Love your enemies, do good to those who hate you, And as you would that people should do to you, do you also to them likewise. For if you love them which love you, what thanks have you? For sinners also love those that love them. And if you do good to them who do good to you, what thanks have you? For sinners also do even the same.'

Yeshuah taught right action in a more positive way and yet it can be much more challenging.

How difficult it is to love those who hurt us without us being seen as weak, vulnerable or downtrodden. And very often a suitable punishment needs to be delivered by society. This needs to be accomplished without hate or retaliation.

> I have three priceless treasures:
> the first is compassion; the second thrift;
> and the third is that I never want to be ahead of you.

Care for others as much as for yourself; be modest in your acquiring of things; be satisfied with your position in life. If you can practise these three treasures, you can feel comfortable with your ethical practice.

3. Right livelihood:

> You shall not steal.

> Let him who stole steal no more, but rather let him labour,
> working with his hands the thing which is good, so that he
> may have something to give to him who needs.
> Six days you shall labour and do all your work.

Make your week's work a practice of dedication to the divine. Find work which is ethically positive so that it hurts no person or creature. Work which harms others harms ourselves - what goes around comes around. This is not as straightforward as it seems in a society as complex as ours. Our responsibility is so much more complicated especially when we expand our reflections to the environment.

In the way of righteousness is life, and in that pathway
there is no death.

*The way of ethics: right speech, action and livelihood.
There can be no spiritual development without a basis
of good ethical practice. In short:*

Love your enemies, bless those who curse you, do good to
those who hate you, and pray for those who spitefully use
you and persecute you, so that you may become children of
your Father in Heaven.
Then you will be complete, even as your Father in Heaven
is complete.

Meditation

My mouth shall speak of wisdom; and the meditation of
my heart shall be of understanding.

4. Right effort / mental discipline:

As the hart pants after the streams of water, so pants my
soul after God, the ĕlôhîym. My soul thirsts for God, for the
living God, אל 'êl.
I will praise you, O LORD, יהוה , with my whole heart;

*As animals long for water to quench their thirst, so do
I long for a connection with and knowledge of God,
ĕlôhîym or 'êl. In whatever form we envisage the sacred
– ĕlôhîym or 'êl, God, Allah, Universal Spirit, יהוה,
enlightenment – we thirst for its presence.
I pursue gnosis with the whole heart, the source of the
soul.*

Blessed are they which do hunger and thirst after righteousness.

May I have the intention to produce and perfect good states of mind while I remove bad and unwholesome states of mind.

5. Right mindfulness:

Blessed is the one whose delight is in the law of יהוה yehôvâh, in which one meditates day and night.

Be mindful of body - kaya, feelings - vedana, mind - citta and thoughts - dhamma. Hold the good things within your minds, resist the bad. This way is not easy; it takes practice and diligence but, as Yeshua said,

Blessed are they who do his commandments that they may have the right to the tree of life ...
Enter in at the strait gate ... the gate is strait, the way is narrow, which leads to life, and few there are who find it.

6. Right concentration:

My mouth shall speak of wisdom; and the meditation of my heart shall be of understanding.

Let there be no thoughts of suffering, ill-will, laziness, doubt: negative thoughts reduce to nothing. Then all intellectual thoughts disappear: no planning, desire, contemplation, mental discourse - the mind becomes one-pointed. Feelings of joy and pleasure are also relinquished resulting in an ambience of equanimity. Positive thoughts have also disappeared. Only pure equanimity and awareness remain.

Blessed are the pure in heart: for they shall see God.

It is simple:
if no-one wants anything for themselves, then there can be peace and all things will know peace, the way music ends in peace.

Wisdom

Value littleness. This is Wisdom.
To bend like a reed in the wind, that is real strength.
Use your mind, but stay close to the light
and it will lengthen its glow right through your life.

Stay close to the Light. Say little, do little but do enough. Work to sustain one's life but be satisfied without desiring more, and more. Think little - meditate. Let the ray of light flow through you to enlighten those around you.

7. Right View:

The Four Noble Truths:
        dukkha - suffering
        samudaya - cause
        nirodha - cessation
        marga — path

The Buddha thought that all is suffering. The rich worry they will lose their wealth and stability; the poor worry they will never gain it. The cause of suffering, samudaya, is desire.

There is a way to end desire, nirodha, and therefore suffering. The Noble Eightfold Path or marga is the means to end the dukkha inherent in life.

> The one who walks uprightly, and works righteousness, and speaks the truth in his heart.

That is, walk silently, in the heart not in the head or the mouth.
Live the truth; work the truth; speak the truth silently.
Know without words - pativedha - without names or labels. Pure experience.

8. Right Resolve:

> Let the words of my mouth, and the meditation of my heart, be acceptable in your sight, O Lord, my strength, and my redeemer.

May my intention be selfless: to walk with the divine and meditate upon His ways and truth with no thought of benefit to myself.

What is good;
> And what does the Lord require of you?
> ... to walk humbly with your God

God is Spirit: and they that worship him must worship him in spirit and in truth.

The Noble Eightfold Path is a Path which guides, supports and challenges us but, as we walk it, we feel the change that takes place within us. Anger and worries settle; love and concern for others grows; and we become closer to God in whichever way we envision the divine.

The fruits of the Spirit that are promised to us are love, joy, peace, long-suffering, gentleness, goodness, faith, meekness, temperance, and these will grow within us as we make the journey along The Noble Eightfold Path.

A Musician's Kybalion – the Seven Principles of Truth

Music is the creation of the spiritual out of the material
Take the elements of the earth
Mix them with water
Add fire as energy and the breath of air
and we have the human voice
the most basic yet supreme of musical instruments
Take the wood from an earth tree containing its lifeblood sap
Work the body of the wood with the fire of energy
until it contains a lung full of air
Listen to the soul as fiddle bow is drawn over strings of pure potential spirit
The instrument sings of the joys of existence ...

... sings of the joys of earthly choirs celebrating life below
echoing the harmonies of heavenly choirs above
All creation worships the Holy One
and, as if by magic, the lower entrains the higher
and the higher realms, the lower
until both sing a pure song of Oneness
We are never alone

Who can know the gift our singing gives to the sacred?
Or who can understand the love we receive in reflection?
The Holy is within us and we are within the Holy ...

... our energies vibrate in perfect unity.
Vibration brings resonance brings sound
The oscillating air waves resound in music
The higher the vibration, the higher the sound
The lower the vibration, the lower the sound
Everything has opposites, everything has duality ...

... everything is on a continuum
Sound changes only in its frequency of vibration
All sounds are intrinsically the same
High sounds, low sounds are similar in nature
Opposites are the same in nature, but different in degree
High, low; good, evil; truth, untruth; love, hate
Opposites are the same in nature, but different in degree
Opposites vibrate in perfect motion ...

... and move in perfect harmony
Nothing in life stands still

rise and fall, in and out, everything has its tides
The ebb and flow of life
in advance or retreat; it cannot stand still
Sound moves; melody and harmony
It cannot stay still
One note leads to another in ordered circumstance
One chord leads to another in the inevitable pursuit ...

... of cadential punctuation
Nothing is left to chance
One follows five as confidently as four precedes five
A multitude of possibilities in a confluence of time and
motion
One thing leads to another
One note follows another as one chord precedes
another
in a ceaseless round of dependent causation
Four, five, one
All paradoxes can be reconciled ...

... four, five, one
a progression through space and time
All paradoxes can be reconciled
All in all, female in male, male in female
The One in both; both in the One

Everything has femaleness, everything has maleness
perseverance and strength, wisdom and compassion
the composed and the spontaneous
Sound and silence
Sound - the creation of patterns of energy that feed
the soul
Music - the creation of the spiritual out of the material.

Ik Omkar

Ik Omkar	One God
Satte naam	Truth is His Name
Kartaa purakh	Supreme Creator
Nirbao Nirvair	Fearless One, Love unbounded
Akaal moorate	Eternal, transcendent
Ajoonee saibhang	Ever present
Gurprasaade	Lord by Thy grace

Ik Omkar: One God,
Omkar, the sound of Om, the sound with no words
One God, Sophia, Krishna, Yahwey, Aloha, Allah,
Goddess, Kali, Brahma ...

Satte naam: Truth is his name
Truth which is both true and not true, the meaning
behind the words are true, the physical / scientific
facts may not be literally true.
In Sanskrit satte is related to both sat and satya. Sat
describes existentiality, beingness; satya means truth
and validity. His name is both the ultimate existence
and the ultimate truth.
His name is Omkar, the silent Om, the only name of
God given by the divine not by mankind. Chant and
meditate on Omkar and the practice becomes the
silent Om. Chant and meditate on the Hebrew Elohim
and Yahwey or the Islamic Allah and the practice

43

becomes the silent Om: the unstruck sound, the anahat naad.

Satte — the mind of satya and the heart of sat; satya alone creates science, sat alone allows the creativity of the arts, painting, music ... Combine the two and there is the Omkar, the divine.

His name, Omkar, is the divine

Kartaa purakh: supreme creator

God is the creator throughout time, in the past, present, and continuing in the future. Furthermore, He remains as a presence within His creations. On the seventh day, He rested — within His creation. God is inseparable from His creation as the dance is inseparable from the dancer. Nataraj, an emanation of Shiva, is a depiction of this relationship between the creator / created and the dancer / dance. Shiva, the destroyer aspect of God, thus has the potential for renewed creation within him. We have the seed within us of the divine creator; it is up to us to find and nurture it.

Nirbao Nirvair: fearless One, love unlimited

God is Ik Omkar — One God. Fear involves the Other. The duality of the material world, body and soul, enables the presence of fear. God has no duality and, therefore, no fear. Realise the interconnectedness of all creation, the oneness, and fear will dissolve away. God fears nothing as he is the undivided One seeing all creation as a unified whole. His love is unlimited to all his creation.

Akaal moorate: eternal, transcendent

With God, there is no death, no limit in space

Only humans are aware of their own death; is this what we gained in the Garden of Eden – the Knowledge of the Good of Life and the Evil of Death?
Change happens in a dualistic world: we measure change using time. If we don't look at and measure change, we don't have time. As humans, it is not possible not to see the world so we always have time.
We are beginning to understand that it is by looking and participating in reality that we create it:
Consciousness is not an observer in the dynamics of the universe: it is an active participant.
And, it is when we look that we inevitably destroy through inescapable change in this material world. Like Schroedinger's cat, when we open the box and look, we will find it - dead or alive.
But God is an integral part of his creation and so cannot look and see change in the materialistic sense so, for Him, time does not exist. He is eternal, outside the realm of time, transcendent, as He is outside time but also imminent as He is a part of His creation.

Ajoonee saibhang: ever present
Immanent, the dance within the dancer, the music within the musician, the being within the creation.
It is this inner being, timeless and blessed, that we may attain through meditation – a taste of the spiritual

Gurprasaade: Lord, by thy grace
By and through the grace of the guru, the master. In Sikhism, this is Guru Nanak, the perfect teacher for his time and place, fifteenth to sixteenth century India.
In Christianity, we attain our connection with God through His grace and through His Son, Yeshua and with the help of the Holy Spirit, God's energy within the world and Divine Wisdom, Holy Sophia.

Ik Omkar

What if ...

The scribes of past times are thought to have made occasional errors in their copying of old manuscripts. Is it possible that this is one such error?

Thorn in Aramaic is ܟܘܒܐ pronounced 'kuba'.

Love in Aramaic is ܚܘܒܐ pronounced 'huba'.

The written difference is one letter: ܟ or ܚ and the sound of the letters is very similar.

What if the 'crown of thorns' was a copyist's error somewhere in the past and we should read a 'crown of love'?

Would the soldiers have crowned him with love? To mock him? Not only was Yeshua called King of the Jews but as a king or emperor who ruled through love; one who they would have seen as weak and laughable.

Yeshua taught love and tolerance. Is the crown of thorns / love an Aramaic pun on words?

How would this have changed the way the artists were to portray Yeshua in the following two thousand years?

A crown of thorns allows for images showing sorrow, pathos, suffering, blood; an inward-looking approach to life inducing feelings of martyrdom and self-denial. It shows one who was to be pitied, who could be viewed as a sacrifice to atone for our wrongdoing. This image results in sadness and guilt.

How could a crown of love be shown by artists? A halo with rays of love? What effect would this image have had on the developing Christian church? Would it engender fellowship between peoples? Love, understanding, connection? The faith would become one of joy, love, compassion, connection...

What if the crown was made of love?

A Dark Night ~ St. John of the Cross

During a dark night,
with longing, enflamed in love,
oh, blessèd grace,
I left unnoticed,
my house being now calm.

In darkness and safety,
by the secret measure, disguised,
oh, blessèd grace,
in darkness and desirable
I am in my peaceful house.

In the blessèd night,
in secret, I was unseen by anyone
nor did I see anything,
without other light or guide
except that which burned in my heart.

This light guided me
more truly than the midday sun
to where He was awaiting me,
He whom I knew well,
to the place where no-one appeared.

Oh, guiding night,
Oh, night kinder than the sunrise,
Oh, night that brings together
The Belovéd with the beloved,
the beloved transformed in the Belovéd.

On my flowery breast,
which is kept wholly for Him alone,
there He stayed sleeping,
and I gave Him gifts,
and the cedars' fanning created a breeze.

The breeze blew softly from the battlements,
as I parted his hair,
while with its calm hand
it wounded my neck
and all my senses ceased.

I was left, forgotten,
my face leaning on the Belovéd.
Everything stopped, and I was left, alone,
leaving my cares
forgotten among the lilies.

The Spiritual Way
according to
The Ten Ox Herding Images & The Dark Night

1. Searching for the ox

High mountains, deep waters,
and a dense jungle of grass,
the way remains unclear!

The Dark Night
The despair of feeling lost.
What am I missing?
Where am I?
What am I looking for?

2. Seeing the footprints

But here and there are footprints.
Is this the right path?

Oh! blesséd grace!
Is this the true way?

3. Seeing the ox   4. Catching the ox

Is this what I am looking for?
I will catch the ox and tame it.
His fiery nature is hard to control.
I feel dragged here and there
and stray through unknown places.

Oh! blesséd grace!
I will catch my thoughts
and subdue my mind.
I try many ways but
this is The Way.

5. Tending the ox   6. Riding the ox back home

Afraid the ox may fall into a dangerous path,
I hold it tight and contain its wanderings
The ox is subdued.
I go home peacefully.

...my house being now calm
In the secrecy of my heart - mind
I am now still and calm.
I return in peace.

7. Forgetting the ox, the ox herder rests alone

Bright moon, cool wind
sitting all alone,
the ox has gone away.

Oh! blesséd grace!
In secret, I meditate,
I am unseen and I see nothing,
with no other light or guide
except that which burns in my heart.

8. The ox and the ox herder are both forgotten

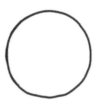

You cheerfully come and go.
How could you not always laugh?
You are fully present; the ox rests.

I was left, forgotten,
leaving my cares among the lilies.
Alone but not alone,
everything stops.
I am fully present; my mind rests.

9. Returning to the Origin 10. Entering the world

The mountains and water are just as they are!
Ragged and bare foot, you approach the market and
the streets.
Even covered in dust, why would the laughter cease?

Oh! bléssed grace!
I forget myself and,
laying my face on my Belovéd,
everything stops.
I leave my cares
forgotten among the lilies.

The bees and butterflies are happy
because flowers have bloomed
on a withered tree.

Oh! bléssed grace
which has re-united
the lost one with the Lord

We yearn for meaning in life. Where can we find it? It is not until we actively search, that we will find it. We are permitted this dark night of unknowing as it encourages us to explore all possibilities and finally pursue our chosen way.

We follow where the track leads and realise that it leads to our inner self, our mind, which is like a stubborn, erratic ox. At first it drags us along but, with effort, we learn to control it and then lead it. Similarly, our mind – heart is wayward and stubborn but with effort this also can be constrained and directed to more meaningful thoughts.

At last, we can ride the Dark Nights of both the senses and the soul knowing that we shall make progress in our search.

We sit in meditation; the mind is at rest.

The practice is accomplished.

Everything is one: emptiness is form and form is emptiness.

Emptiness alone implies separation but the world is still present. We realise integration; we are in the world and open to it yet not suffering from or being overwhelmed by it.

Like Putei, the laughing Buddha, we can laugh and feel filled with the blessings of the world. And, like Putei, we carry a bag of wisdom and compassion with which to help our fellow travellers.

Sophia is calling

Sophia is calling. Listen to her; pursue Wisdom and find happiness and peace.
Contemplating the divine, YHVH, gives wisdom, knowledge, and understanding of God, the Elohim.

Yah - breathe in energy from above

Heh - move the energy down and through the arms

Vah - breathe in energy from above

Heh - move the energy through and down the legs to the ground

Bring divine energy from Heaven to Earth

and rest in the imminence of the Divine

Notes on the texts

Unfortunately, the ideas in these texts have developed over many years' reading and contemplating so appropriate references are frequently lost in the mists of time and an imperfect memory. Those that are remembered or rediscovered are included here.

You should find the references here in the correct order for the quotations which are in this font in the text. The Reader can probably apply them appropriately but, if not, it is not disadvantageous. They are here to achieve academic rigour in an unacademic way. My thoughts are in this font.

The Biblical quotations are based on the King James Version retranslated by the author for ease of reading or increased accuracy. They are in Hebrew and Aramaic scripts when necessary.

A Prayer of Dedication

Behold, the servant ... Luke 1:38 in Aramaic and Hebrew script

A Story of Noah

Based on Genesis 6:8
Please note: This was conceived during my first one hour of allowed exercise at the start of the Isolation in 2020. As I walked the beach in solitude - with a few other people in solitude - I remembered the story of Noah and its relevance to the current time.

In case of mis-understanding this writing:

I do not believe that God sent this virus to punish humanity.

In Genesis 6, Noah was the only good person and God sent the flood to wipe out an errant humanity but He saved Noah. This was a very crude way of describing cause and effect: do wrong and you will be punished.

This version is an attempt to show that we gain the results of our own actions; we reap what we sow. Damage to the environment will result in damage within the environment.
I don't believe in conspiracy theories. We probably enabled this virus to enter humans by something as simple as harvesting bat manure uncleanly. If this is so, it is not the fault of the bats or of any other creature similarly blamed.
Whatever the cause, the results have been disastrous.
I have tried to describe the damage this has caused to our young ones who have had negative experiences in the aim of protecting the older and more vulnerable amongst us.
May we look to the future and work towards never letting this happen again.

My Creed

The Smaragdine or Emerald Tablet which includes the words, 'That which is above is from that which is below, and that which is below is from that which is above,'

The Lord's Prayer

Matthew 6:9b

Creation 1

Genesis 1 In the beginning, Beresheit (or berê'shîyth בְּרֵאשִׁית) derives from an unused root apparently meaning to shake; the head (as most easily shaken), whether literally or figuratively (in many applications, of place, time, rank, etc.): - band, beginning, cap — Strong
This can be translated as, 'in the turning of the head', or finding a new focus ...

בָּרָא bârâ - to create as in the creation of Beriah, one of the Qabalistic four worlds. As Stephen Pope comments, 'Neither concept (Creation or Beriah) denotes the physical universe, nor is the creation a past event: it is a continual outpouring from the eternal Now' (Pope, 2011, Patterns of Creation p 14)

The name elôhîym comes from elôahh אֱלוֹהַּ a grammatically feminine noun with a masculine plural ending יִם îym.

Emptiness. Vacuité. Śūnyatā — terms central to Buddhism

Creation 2

Genesis 2:5-7; 8-9; 15; 16, 17; 21-23;
Genesis 3 abridged and partly re-translated
יְהוָה אֱלֹהִים yehôvâh elôhîym
אֱלֹהִים elôhîym
The three lower worlds of Jewish thought derive from the words describing creation: created בָּרָא bârâ' - Beriah; formed יָצַר yâtsar – Yetzirah, made עָשָׂה 'âśâh Assiyah. Only Atzilut is not stated verbally.

The Four Holy Truths of Job

In the north-eastern area of India, the Buddha's birthplace, poverty, hunger, thirst and disease were the lived experience of most of the population. Siddharta Gautama, however, was born into a wealthy, powerful family with none of these deprivations and yet he still found life to be unsatisfactory. His father was fearful that he would become a spiritual leader and not a political leader and protected Him from knowledge of the world outside his palace. Siddharta found his lack of knowledge and understanding to be disturbing and escaped the palace to discover the deeper truths of existence. This is what he found: a worn-out old man, a sick man, a corpse and a saffron robed spiritual *samana*, who seemed to be at peace with the world. He chose to follow the *samana's* way and discovered the Four Holy Truths:

1. Life is suffering and consists of much suffering or dukkha.
Birth, ageing, ill health and death are suffering. Sorrow and despair are suffering.
Attachment to and separation from both what one likes and what one dislikes is suffering.
2. It is desire, taṇhā, which causes suffering when one tries to acquire cravings or remove unwanted experiences. Such desire results in war, famine, ecological damage and so on.
3. There is a solution to desire and its outcomes: the cessation, nirodha, of attachment resulting in nibbāna, enlightenment.
4. The Eightfold Path leads to the extinction of dukkha and taṇhā resulting in nirodha and ultimately, nibbāna.

Sophia's Noble Eightfold Path

Technically the title should be translated as the Eightfold Path for the Noble Ones; this title is retained as it is better known.

Source texts include the Dīgha Nikāya, the Long Discourses of the Buddha, 22, Mahāsatipatthāna Sutta, 21

Proverbs 3: 13, 15, 17

אדם' âdâm: a person, an individual of a species not a masculine person v 13

חכמה chokmâh wisdom, a feminine noun hence she in v 15

דרך derek a way, figuratively a path through life v 17

Digha Nikaya, The Long Discourses of the Buddha, Mahagovinda Sutta, 19:61

The eight paths designed to develop compassion (karuna) and wisdom (panna) divide into three sections:

1. Ethics - right speech, right action, right livelihood
2. Meditation - right effort, right mindfulness, right concentration
3. Wisdom – right view, right resolve

1. Ethics: sila Matt 7:12

See also Psalm 40:8; Ezekiel 36:27

1. right speech samma vaca: Deut 5:11, 20, Matt 5:9, Tao Te Ching 17, 23
2. right action samma kammanta: Deut 5:17 - 19; Deut 5:7 - 9; Luke 6:27,31-33; Tao Te Ching 67

3. right livelihood   samma ajiva: Deut 6:19,
   Eph 4:28, Pro 12:28, Matt 5:44
   τέλειος teleios complete Matt 5:48
   See also Deut 5:13

2. Meditation / right mind / mindfulness: samadhi
   Psa 49:3
   4. right effort Psa 42:1,2; Psa 9:1; Matt 5:6
   5. right mindfulness Psa 1:1,2
   the four Buddhist foci of mindfulness: body -
   kaya, feelings - vedana, mind - citta and
   thoughts - dhamma
   Rev 22:14, Matt 7:13,14
   6. right samadhi / concentration Psa 49:3;
      Matt 5:8; Tao Te Ching 37;

3. Wisdom: panna Tao Te Ching 52;
       7. right view ditthi - in Buddhism there are
two sorts of understanding. Firstly, knowledge, an
accumulated memory, an intellectual grasping of a
subject according to certain given data known as
anubodha. Meditation aims for the second — a deep
understanding or   pativedha, seeing a thing in its true
nature, without name and label. This penetration is
possible only when the mind is free from all impurities
and is fully developed through meditation.
       Psa 15:2;
       8. right resolve sankappa Psa 19:14; Micah
6:6-8
       See also: John 4:24
       Gal 5:22, 23

A Musician's Kybalion - the Seven Principles of Truth

See The Kybalion on Wikipedia

1 The Principle of Mentalism - the material world is made of spirit, created by the All

2 The Principle of Correspondence - as above so below; as below so above

3 The Principle of Vibration - all is vibration

4 The Principle of Polarity - everything is dual; everything has opposites

5 The Principle of Rhythm - everything flows

6 The Principle of Cause and Effect - there is no such thing as chance

7 The Principle of Gender - everything contains the Masculine and Feminine Principles

... of cadential punctuation: IV, V, I, conventional theory of harmony

Ik Omkar

The first guru, Guru Nanak Dev Ji, instituted the Sikh tradition of singing shabads or hymns as a way to approach the divine. The Ik Omkar begins one such shabad, the Japji. The ninth guru, Guru Tegh Bahadur, was executed with three of his followers in 1675. This strengthened the decision of the tenth guru to terminate the succession. This Guru Gobind Singh did just that and made the spiritual text, the Sri Guru Granth Sahib (the SGGS) the last and continuing guru. He also instigated the Khalsa, the community of pure believers, by baptising the Five Pure Men with water and sugar. They then baptised him as the sixth member of the community which continues to this day.

Transliterations vary; this is taken from *The True Name*, talks on Japji by Osho, Hind Pocket Books Pvt Ltd, 1980

Japji is Nanak's first spoken words after emerging from the river when he achieved union with the divine. It begins the SGGS.

For meditating on the Hebrew Elohim and Yahwey see *The Beatitudes in Aramaic*, Kite C , 2021, p 59

Do animals have an understanding of their own deaths? There are those that grieve the loss of their partners, for example, our ape cousins and many birds which mate for life

Consciousness quotation: Reanney D, *The Death of Forever*, 1991, Souvenir Press p 26

Nanak attained God by singing to him; Nanak's quest is very unusual – his path was decorated with songs. The first thing to be realised is that Nanak practised no austerities or meditation or yoga; he only sang, and singing, he arrived. He sang with all his heart and soul, so much so that his singing became meditation; his singing became his purification and his yoga.

Osho, *The True Name*, 1980, Hind Pocket Books Pvt Ltd, p 10

What if ...

The Aramaic testaments Mark (15:17) and John (19:2,5) have ܟܘܒܐ 'kuba' as thorns.

Matthew (27:29) has ܟܘܒܐ 'awznaye' thorns.

The Greek gospels have ἀκάνθινος 'akanthinos' thorny, of thorns in Mark and John; Matthew has ἄκανθα 'akantha', a thorn.

The Greek for love is ἀγαπάω 'agapaō'. The pun on words does not occur in Greek.

Further to this, a Bible search on thorn includes a reference to 2 Corinthians 12:7 translated as 'a thorn for my flesh'. The Greek uses σκόλοψ 'skolops', defined as 'withered at the front, a point or prickle, figuratively a bodily annoyance or disability, a thorn'.

The Aramaic Peshitta* has ܪܠܟܘܐ ܡܐܪܠܐ , a 'malakeh d'satana', a messenger of Satan.
*https://theholyaramaicscriptures.weebly.com

The source texts for the Bible can vary considerably creating differing translations.

A Dark Night

A poem written by St John of the Cross while he was in prison.

The translation is by the author.

The Spiritual Way

See Wikipedia Ten Bulls for the ten ox herding images and further information
See Dark Night of the Soul at carmelitemonks.org for
or K Kavanaugh & O Rodriguez, 2017, *The Collected Works of St John of the Cross*
The texts have been translated / adapted by the author.
See www.paulwagner.com/the-heart-sutra-english-sanskrit/ for *The Heart Sutra* or *Prajnaparamita Sutra*: 'Form does not differ from emptiness; emptiness does not differ from form. Form itself is emptiness; emptiness itself is form.'

Glossary of Hebrew terms

'âbad עבד to dress, work

'âdâm אדם man

aᵈâmâh אֲדָמָה ground

arets ארץ earth

'âśâh עשׂה made

banah הנב built

bârâ' ברא created

berê'shîyth בראשית in the beginning

binah בִּין understanding

chavvâh חוּה Eve, life-giver

chokmâh חָכְמָה wisdom

da'at דַעַת knowledge

'êl אל God

eᵉlôahh אֱלוֹהַ God

eᵉlôhîym אֱלֹהִים the Elohim, the great God

'ishshâh אשׁה woman

îym ים masculine plural suffix

kâbash כבשׁ subdue

73

îysh אִישׁ man

nâphach נפח breathed

nephesh נפשׁ soul

neshâmâh נשׁמה breath

râdâh רדה have dominion

shâmar שׁמ ר to keep, guard

yâtsar יצר formed

yehôvâh יהוה LORD

yehôvâh elôhîym יהוה אלהים the LORD God

Where two or three are gathered together in my name, there am I in the midst of them.

As writer and reader unite in pursuing Wisdom, may the Divine One be with us and may the path to peace be strengthened.

Lightning Source UK Ltd.
Milton Keynes UK
UKHW020703110422
401395UK00008B/205